Changing The Seen
and
Shaping The Unseen

by
Charles Capps

HARRISON HOUSE
Tulsa, Oklahoma

Unless otherwise indicated,
all Scripture quotations are from
the *King James Version* of the Bible.

Verses marked *Amplified* are taken from
The Amplified Bible, New Testament. © 1954, 1958
by The Lockman Foundation,
La Habra, California,
Used by permission.

11th Printing
Over 102,000 in Print

Changing The Seen and Shaping The Unseen
ISBN 0-89274-220-8
(formerly ISBN 0-89274-165-1)
Copyright © 1980, 1981 by Charles Capps
P. O. Box 69
England, Arkansas 72046

Published by Harrison House, Inc.
P. O. Box 35035
Tulsa, Oklahoma 74153

Contents

1

Looking At The Unseen

Seen things have become so real to some people that they have forgotten about the unseen.

We live in a world of the natural. We rub shoulders with the physical day after day until the unseen realm seems unreal. We are almost tempted to believe it doesn't exist!

But Paul said:

For our light affliction, which is but for a moment, worketh for us a far more exceeding and eternal weight of glory;

While we look not at the things which are seen, but at the things which are not seen: for the things which are seen are temporal; but the things which are not seen are eternal.

2 Corinthians 4:17,18

These words almost cause us to think the Apostle Paul had lost his mind when he said, *Look not at the things which are seen.* How in the world can you look at something you can't see?

Paul is talking about unseen principles: the principles of God's Word which are actually spiritual law — spiritual forces that are unseen. These are eternal forces which always work when you set them in motion.

Notice what the Apostle Paul said: *For our light affliction, which is but for a moment, worketh for us a far more exceeding and eternal weight of glory; While we look not at the things which are seen . . . .*

In other words, if you're looking only at seen things, things of the natural, then the affliction will not work an exceeding weight of glory in you: It will work only *while* you're looking at things which are *not seen.*

You must shift over into the realm of spiritual law and begin to look at things which are not seen with the natural eye. **You look at things which are not seen with the eye of the spirit — the eye of faith.**

Notice Paul didn't say, "*All* affliction will work a far exceeding weight of glory." He said it would happen only while you're looking at *things which are not seen.*

Ask yourself the question: "What are the *things which are not seen?*"

If you're having financial problems and the bank statement comes back in red ink, then the thing that is *not* seen is the bankbook balancing or your need being met.

The thing that *is* seen is *lack.* Paul said that pressure will work for you an exceeding eternal weight of glory *if you will look* at things that are *not seen.* It is actually the *looking at the unseen* that brings the glory, not the pressure of the affliction.

This agrees with what he said in Philippians 4:8: *Finally, brethren, whatsoever things are true, whatsoever things are honest, whatsoever things are just, whatsoever things are pure, whatsoever things are lovely, whatsoever things are of good report; if there be any virtue, and if there be any praise, think on these things.*

In other words, get your mind off the problem and begin to think on the things that are *not seen* — the things you desire, the things you don't see with your physical eye. You must learn to see the answer by the *eye of faith.*

The word *temporal* means "subject to change." Things you are seeing with the physical, natural eye are always subject to change through spiritual law.

So many times what we see with our physical eye does not agree with the Word of God, the promises of God. **The world's system shapes the seen things around us.** They seem to be very real, and they *are* real; but the Word of God says that *they are subject to change!*

God's Word is the establishing force of the image of unseen things. We should not allow circumstances and the cares of life to create images within us. Take God's Word and change things that are seen — the things you don't desire — into things that you do desire.

8

In this book, I want to show you how to change the seen and shape the unseen.

Wrong Assumptions

Words produce images inside us; but sometimes we get these images by making wrong assumptions. Let me give you an example.

During a certain meeting, the Lord had been dealing with me about teaching on this subject of wrong assumptions producing false images. One night after the meeting, the man who took me to the motel was driving a gray-colored Grand Prix.

The next morning when he came to pick me up, he went out ahead of me to take my bags to the car. He told me he was parked down on the left.

I walked out and looked to the left. Seeing a car that looked like his, I started walking toward it. I heard someone blow his horn at me; but when I turned around, I saw a gold-colored Cadillac. Looking for the Grand Prix I walked on. The man sounded his horn again.

Finally, when he backed up and blew the horn again, I looked to see who was in the Cadillac. It was my man.

I had an image of him sitting in a Grand Prix. Because I was looking for a Grand Prix, I missed him! The car had been right in front of me all the time, but I hadn't paid any attention to it. I just walked right by it.

Because we have not *shaped the unseen* within us, we miss it. We walk by it. We let it go. Sometimes God sets it before us; but because we've never shaped the image of the unseen within us, we keep pushing it out of the way, looking for something else. We're so wrapped up in what is seen that we fail to see the unseen.

Creating Right Images

We need to recognize one thing: **It is God's Word that will establish the image of the unseen within us.** We should not allow circumstances or the cares of this life to create images within us. *What the Word says* should create the image.

10

Let me paraphrase what Paul said in 2 Corinthians 4:18: "If you don't get rid of that image of looking at the seen, and produce another image inside you, then the afflictions of life will not work in you an eternal weight of glory. But they will, *if* you're looking at the things that are not seen."

We should take God's Word and change the things that are seen — things we don't desire — into the things that we do desire.

Someone said, "I can plainly see my financial situation. I can plainly see the red ink on my bank statement."

Those are things you can see. The exceeding eternal weight of glory will be brought into place by looking at the unseen. Notice, it is not the affliction that brought glory, but concentrating on the unseen. The unseen is from the spirit world. Spiritual forces are released by God's Word being spoken.

Unseen things are shaped by the Word of God. For example, the Word says:

11

Give, and it shall be given unto you; good measure, pressed down, and shaken together, and running over, shall men give into your bosom. For with the same measure that ye mete withal it shall be measured to you again.

Luke 6:38

He which soweth bountifully shall reap also bountifully.

2 Corinthians 9:6

My God shall supply all your need according to his riches in glory by Christ Jesus.

Philippians 4:19

You may not see these things now with your physical eye, but they are very real. They are shaped by *God's Word* and *your confession!* When you look around, you see lack; but God's Word says, *Give, and it shall be given . . . He which soweth bountifully shall also reap bountifully.*

You change the seen with God's Word. You shape the unseen by calling things that are not as though they were. (Rom. 4:17.)

2

Faith Is Unseen

But God hath chosen the foolish things of the world to confound the wise; and God hath chosen the weak things of the world to confound the things which are mighty;

And base things of the world, and things which are despised, hath God chosen, yea, and things which are not, to bring to nought things that are.

1 Corinthians 1:27,28

Look at the same passage in *The Amplified Bible:*

"[No,] for God selected — deliberately chose — what in the world is foolish to put the wise to shame, and what the world calls weak to put the strong to shame.

"And God also selected — deliberately chose — [what] in the world [is] lowborn and insignificant, and branded and treated with contempt, even the things that are nothing, that He might depose and bring to nothing the things that are."

God has chosen things that are not to bring to naught things that are! He is simply talking about things not revealed to the physical senses.

Hebrews 11:1 tells us: *Faith is the substance of things hoped for, the evidence of things not seen.*

Faith is the substance, the raw material. One translation says that faith is giving substance to things hoped for, to what you desire and what is not yet manifested to the physical senses.

Faith is the substance that God used to create the universe, and He transported that faith with His words. God used His words as containers to transport His faith out there into the vast nothingness, into the darkness.

He said, "Light, be!" (Gen. 1:3.)

And light was!

When there was nothing but darkness, God took the Word *light* and spoke it into existence. He took that which *was* *not* and brought to naught that which *was*!

In Genesis 1:26,27 we are told that God created man in His own image and likeness. Therefore, man is capable of taking those things which are not and bringing to naught those things which are! He is capable of taking things that are not revealed to the physical senses and bringing to naught things that are revealed to the physical senses.

Faith is the substance of things, but you can't *see* faith. Faith is a spiritual force. You can't see my faith. For example: What if my wife and I got in our airplane to go on a trip, but after looking out the windows, decided we couldn't go because we didn't see any lift on the wings?

Or what if, after getting the airplane up to 70 miles an hour on the runway, I cut the engines because I didn't see any air out the window?

That way of thinking is dumb, isn't it? You can't see lift on a wing. A lift is an unseen force produced by the unseen air flowing over the wing.

You can't see air. You can't feel it or hear it; so there must not be any there. Right? Wrong!

God chose the things that you couldn't see to bring to naught the things you could see. When you realize these laws work and you begin to work them, then you can supersede other laws.

The law of thrust and lift will supersede the law of gravity. The law of thrust and lift doesn't do away with the law of gravity; gravity is still working. But we're taking the things that are *not seen* and causing the things that *are seen* to come to naught.

An airplane can be seen. You can see it, touch it, and feel it. If you bit into it, you could taste it.

Naturally speaking, the airplane is too heavy to fly. It weighs about two tons when empty; but because of the law of lift, it can fly.

For years, men didn't know anything about that law. But when you understand these laws and set them in motion, one law has to give way to the other. Things that are not seen put to naught things that are seen, and my airplane flies like a bird, up to 31,000 feet.

You don't supersede one law with another by violating God's laws. First, you have to find out how they work; then you have to cooperate with them.

Operating according to God's laws causes you to be able to shape things that don't seem to be — the unseen — into a workable situation.

3

Changing The Seen

An excellent example of changing the seen and shaping the unseen is shown in the life of Abraham.

Therefore it is of faith, that it might be by grace; to the end the promise might be sure to all the seed; not to that only which is of the law, but to that also which is of the faith of Abraham; who is the father of us all,

(As it is written, I have made thee a father of many nations,) before him whom he believed, even God, who quickeneth the dead, and calleth those things which be not as though they were.
Romans 4:16,17

Notice, it is God and Abraham who are calling things that are not as though they were. God said, *I have made thee a father of many nations*. Abraham didn't have a child at that time, but the Bible says he believed God, and it was accounted unto him for righteousness. (v. 22.)

This is the way you begin to change the seen and shape the unseen. Abraham called things which were not manifest in the natural realm as though they were — until they were!

Abraham was the man who *against hope believed in hope, that he might become the father of many nations, according to that which was spoken* (v. 18). He was 99 years old, and his wife was 90; but he was *not weak in faith* (v. 19). **He would not consider anything that contradicted what God had spoken.**

Let's notice what God did to bring about what He had said.

Neither shall thy name any more be called Abram, but thy name shall be Abraham; for a father of many nations have I made thee.

And God said unto Abraham, As for Sarai thy wife, thou shalt not call her name Sarai, but Sarah shall her name be.

Genesis 17:5,15

God had promised Abraham something that was absolutely impossible in the natural. Abraham was too old, Sarah was too old; and God does not violate His laws.

So God changed their names! *Abraham* means "father of nations" and *Sarah* means "mother of nations." Every time Sarah stuck her head out the tent door and called *Abraham!* he didn't hear *Abraham!* — he heard *Father of Nations!*

The Bible says, *Faith cometh by hearing, and hearing by the word of God* (Rom. 10:17). God changed the seen and shaped the unseen for Abraham and Sarah by using their own voices!

When Abraham said, "My name is Abraham," he was saying, "I am the Father of Nations." Every time Abraham said *Sarah,* she didn't hear *Sarah;* she heard *Mother of Nations*.

Every time she said, "My name is Sarah," she was saying, "My name is Mother of Nations." She was changing the seen and shaping the unseen with her very own voice.

God's way of changing the seen and establishing the unseen is with *words*. Words produce images in your spirit and in your mind.

The Bible says Sarah received faith to conceive seed. She did it by hearing God's Word for her. When anyone said *Abraham* or *Sarah,* they were saying, *Thus saith the Lord.*

God said, "I *have made* thee (past tense) the father of many nations." The Word says that Abraham believed God, and he went about calling things that were not as though they were. This is the way you begin to shape the unseen.

Faith Always Sees

Abraham did not see with his physical eye that he was the father of many nations. When I talk about shaping the unseen, I'm not talking about something that is unseen in your spirit. You can see things in your spirit as well as with the natural eye.

Sometimes people say, "That fellow just had blind faith." But there's no such thing as *blind faith*. Faith always sees. Faith always knows.

You don't see these things with the natural eye, but you perceive them in your spirit by discerning the Word of God by the Spirit of God within you.

Abraham called things that *were not* (manifest in the natural realm) as though they *were* (manifest in the natural realm) until they *were* (manifest in the natural realm). And the Word says that God did the same thing: He called things that were not as though they were.

Who against hope believed in hope, that he might become the father of many nations, according to that which was spoken . . . (v. 18).

Notice: *according to that which was spoken*. Abraham believed in hope when there was no hope.

Abraham could have said, "Here I am — 99 years old. My hundredth birthday is not far away, and my wife is 90."

He could have begun to look at what was seen and said, "Oh, no! That could never come to pass. That'll never happen.

That must not have been God talking to me. That was just my flesh." (It couldn't have been his flesh because the carnal mind doesn't think that way.) Abraham believed in hope when there was no hope.

Abraham Considered Not His Own Body

And being not weak in faith, he **considered not** *his own body now dead . . .* (v. 19).

If you want to change the seen, the first thing you need to do is *consider not*. Don't consider what you can see to be eternal. Don't consider what you can see to be established because the Word of God says things which are seen are temporal: They are subject to change by the Word of God and your faith.

Abraham believed God: *And being not weak in faith, he* **considered not** *his own body now dead, when he was about an hundred years old, neither yet the deadness of Sarah's womb.* He cast down imaginations and brought them into obedience to the Word of God.

Sometimes you have to cast down *your* imagination. (2 Cor. 10:5.) The devil will use your imagination if you let him.

Several years ago my daughter Annette was out late one night. As I was lying there in bed, I began to think. Immediately, the negative began to form in my mind.

The enemy, through my carnal mind, said, "She's had a wreck. There's been a big rain. She ran off in a ditch and turned over. You've seen her alive for the last time."

As those ideas came forth, I saw a mental vision: I saw the car go off the road and turn over in a ditch of water. Then I saw the water come up over the car. That's the devil's way of coming as an angel of light. (2 Cor. 11:14.)

I said, "No! In the name of Jesus, that doesn't agree with the Word of God. My children are taught of the Lord, and *great is the peace of my children!*" (Is. 54:13.)

About that time, I heard the door slam as she came in.

You must cast down imaginations and bring them into obedience to God's Word.

Renew Your Mind

To get rid of the seen, or what seems to be, you must get your mind and spirit so programmed with the Word of God that you will reject *all* the devil has to offer. Your spirit will scream, *Reject! Reject! It doesn't agree with God's Word!*

Then you begin to shape the unseen by God's Word.

Someone said, "Why should we walk in defeat and in despair when God's Word has been spoken?"

God has already had His say on the subject. The problem is that some don't know what He has said, and that enables the devil to take advantage of them.

We see in Romans 4:20-22 that Abraham wouldn't consider anything except what God said:

He staggered not at the promise of God through unbelief; but was strong in faith, giving glory to God;

And being fully persuaded that, what he (God) *had promised, he was able also to perform,*

And therefore it was imputed to him for righteousness.

The word *righteousness* is an Old English word that means *right standing.* Abraham's faith was considered or imputed to him for right standing with God.

Some might say, "I don't understand it. I don't have any trouble believing God for finances, but I do have trouble believing Him for healing," or vice versa. The same problem may exist in other areas.

When you get your mind renewed to the Word of God concerning prosperity — and realize that it is God's will for you to prosper — then you can operate in that faith. But you can't believe any further than you have knowledge.

You have to get yourself in line with the Word of God in the other areas, too. If you have been taught that healing went out with the apostles and that God doesn't do miracles anymore, then you're inhibited in that area. You're not in right standing with God concerning miracles.

You may be right with God; you may make it to heaven. But in one or more areas you might not be in right standing. It's not imputed to you for right standing because you are believing wrong. You are talking wrong and thinking wrong, because you have been taught wrong. Faith comes by hearing God's Word. (Rom. 10:17.)

Shape The Unseen

Your words are shaping the unseen — daily.

That is why God told Joshua:

This book of the law (the Word of God) *shall not depart out of thy mouth; but thou shalt meditate therein day and night, that thou mayest observe to do according to all that is written therein: for then thou shalt make thy way prosperous, and then thou shalt have good success.*

Joshua 1:8

The word *meditate* is interesting. *Meditate* means "to mutter; to speak to one's self."

In other words, this is saying, "As you confess what God said about your situation, you will make your way prosperous and do wisely in all the affairs of life."

Who was going to make Joshua's way prosperous? Joshua.

How? By shaping the unseen with the words of his mouth.

David's Sword Was In His Mouth

The 17th chapter of 1 Samuel describes David's encounter with Goliath, the giant sent from the Philistines to defeat the men of Israel.

David walked out where the battle was supposed to be; but no one was fighting. They were all afraid! He said, "Is there not a cause?"

This was not a man of war; he was a shepherd boy; but he had learned to **change the seen** and **shape the unseen.**

When he saw the giant, he said, "I'll go fight him. Who is this uncircumcised

Philistine? Who does he think he is to defy the armies of the Living God?"

He just filled himself with God's Word until he couldn't see anything but success. To David, that giant was defeat going somewhere to happen because he was defying the armies of the Living God.

Five times before David *did* anything, *he said what he was going to do* to the giant!

What was he doing? He was **shaping the unseen.**

He could have said, "As big as that guy is, just one swish with that sword and I'll be in two pieces!" He could have thought about all the "what-if's." (Have you ever had a bad case of the *what-if's*? "What if it doesn't work?")

But David didn't get the *what-if's*. **He only spoke what was in agreement with God's Word.** He was shaping the unseen. The only sword that he had was the one in his mouth — the twoedged sword of God's Word.

4

Shut Your Mouth

Sometimes if you're going to change the seen to the unseen, you have to shut your mouth. Take Zacharias, for instance. God sent the angel Gabriel to speak to him.

Gabriel said: *Fear not, Zacharias: for thy prayer is heard; and thy wife Elisabeth shall bear thee a son, and thou shalt call his name John* (Luke 1:13).

Zacharias and Elisabeth had been praying for this. But when God sent the angel with the message that their prayers were going to be answered, Zacharias said, "How do I know you're telling the truth? Give me a sign." (v. 18, paraphrased.)

Gabriel probably thought, *If we don't get this guy's mouth shut, it's not going to work.*

Just picture Zacharias going to Elisabeth. He might have said, "A guy appeared to me who *seemed* to be an angel and said his name was Gabriel. But he said some strange things, and I just don't know. *What if* he wasn't from God?"

They would have thought about it, talked about it, got unbelief stirred up, and the birth of their son would never have come to pass.

God pressed the angel to get Zacharias' mouth shut.

Gabriel said, "All right. I'm going to give you a sign. By this sign you'll know that it'll come to pass. (Not only that, but also he was *insuring* that it *would* come to pass!) You'll be dumb and not able to speak until it happens."

Here you see the wisdom of God. God said, "I'll take the things that are not and bring to naught the things that are." Words that are *not* spoken are much more powerful than words that *are* spoken in unbelief.

Keep God's Secrets

Ten years ago the Spirit of God to me some things that are

happening to me right now; but I didn't tell everyone about it.

When God reveals some things to you, He doesn't intend for you to tell everybody. If you do, they will probably try to talk you out of it.

Joseph's Revelation

Genesis, beginning with chapter 37, describes what happened to Joseph, when he revealed a secret that God had told him. The devil found out about it and tried to stop it from coming to pass; but in spite of all the devil could do, Joseph wouldn't let go of God's Word.

Joseph shaped the unseen things by the Word of God within him. God showed Joseph that he would be above his people; they would be bowing to him. He would be in a position of authority.

His brothers threw him in a well, but he still retained the vision. It didn't look bright down there with the frogs and water moccasins, but he still had God's Word! His brothers sold him into Egypt where his master falsely accused him and put him in jail.

But everywhere they put Joseph, he ended up being the doer of everything that was done. Even though he'd been sold into Egypt, pharaoh promoted him in the kingdom because he had God's favor. He was a Word man.

Somebody may say, "Yes, it was amazing how God led Joseph through all those trials, tests, and problems to get him to the position where he would be in authority."

God did not have to use the devil to get Joseph into a position of authority. *His Word was capable of doing that.* But Joseph told God's secret. God revealed something to him that he had no business sharing with other people.

But in spite of it all, Joseph kept God's Word first place. He changed the seen and shaped the unseen by the Word of God that was revealed to him.

Some Things Are Better Unspoken

God does not intend for us to tell everything He reveals to us.

I've seen some things in my spirit that God has shown me which I haven't even told my wife; so the devil doesn't know about it. When I pray about it, I pray in the Spirit.

The devil sure would like to know what it is because he'd try to head it off. He doesn't know and I'm not going to tell him, even though I could unwittingly, through prayer. Sometimes you give the devil valuable information when you pray. Let me give you an example.

A guy walks down the street. All of a sudden, two thugs jump out, stick a gun in his ribs, and say, "Give us your money!"

He's a man of prayer. Prayer is good for everything, right?

The man throws his hands up in the air and says, "Oh, dear God, don't let them find that hundred-dollar bill I put in my shoe!"

That's dumb! That's not the way to shape things. He's going to get things out of shape.

Sometimes silence is more important than prayer.

5

A Time To Speak,
A Time To Be Silent

The Word of the Lord has been spoken. God's Word is out. God's Word is the final authority on any subject.

To change the seen things, sometimes you must get your mouth in motion.

There are other times, if you're going to change what's seen, you will have to practice the vocabulary of silence.

This is especially true in situations where Satan comes against you so strongly that you can't bring yourself to say the things that are positive or in line with the Word of God. The pressure is on, the circumstance is wild, and all that rises up within you is *against* what God says. You know if you say anything, it will be negative; so don't say anything.

Be quiet before God because His Word has already been spoken. You have confessed it for weeks, but now it's time to be quiet.

Jairus is a good example of keeping quiet after confessing in faith. In the 5th chapter of Mark, verses 22 and 23, Jairus came to Jesus in behalf of his daughter:

Behold, there cometh one of the rulers of the synagogue, Jairus by name; and when he saw him, he fell at his feet,

And besought him greatly, saying, My little daughter lieth at the point of death: I pray thee, come and lay thy hands on her, that she may be healed; and she shall live.

Words of Faith

Jairus said, . . . *and she shall live.* Those are his faith-filled words. He is building a faith image — shaping the unseen. He set the *law of faith* in motion with his *words of faith.*

Follow Jesus, in verses 24-27, as He goes to Jairus' house and see how it worked:

Jesus went with him; and much people followed him, and thronged him.

38

And a certain woman, which had an issue of blood twelve years,

And had suffered many things of many physicians, and had spent all that she had, and was nothing bettered, but rather grew worse,

When she had heard of Jesus, came in the press behind, and touched his garment.

"Grow Worse" Image

Notice what was said of this woman. After spending all she had (indicating she may have been rich at one time) and suffering many things, she *was nothing bettered, but rather grew worse*. No doubt this woman had within her a "grow worse" image.

Many Christians have formed within themselves a "grow worse" image. They never see themselves getting any better. They never see themselves having any more than what they have had because of past experiences.

Perhaps they allowed fear to creep in and cause the circumstances to be as they are. Sometimes it is just a wrong decision they made that brought on the problems. Then the devil said, "These problems are happening because God is teaching you something."

When they believed him, they received that "grow worse" image as being from God the Father. Then they couldn't pray in faith. That image held them in bondage for years because they were deceived by the evil one.

All that time, God in His mercy would have loved to heal them or deliver them if they had released faith in God's deliverance.

Image Change

No doubt that "grow worse" image had hold of the woman in the 5th chapter of Mark. Notice what changed this "grow worse" image into a faith image: *When she had heard of Jesus . . .* (v. 27).

What had she heard about Jesus?

No doubt she heard words that Jesus had spoken. He was going about touching people and saying, "Be healed. Be clean. Go and be whole of your plague."

She heard that these people were instantly healed. Most likely she heard what Jesus had said concerning sickness and oppression of the evil one. (Luke 13:12.) I am sure she heard about the Covenant.

We know she heard about Jesus. Jesus was the Word of God. When she heard about Jesus, she heard the Word. *Faith cometh by hearing, and hearing by the word of God* (Rom. 10:17).

Words Produce Images

When she **heard** these things, they produced faith inside her. They began to change her image. Then she started **changing the seen** and **shaping the unseen.**

How did she do it? **With her words!**

The Amplified Bible says, "She kept saying, If I only touch His garments, I shall be restored to health."

She started down the road to where Jesus was and kept saying, "If I can but touch His clothes, I will be made whole. If I can but touch His clothes, I shall be restored to health. I *shall* be . . . I *shall* be . . . ."

Then her religious head screamed out, *"When* are you going to be healed and restored to health? You don't *look* any better. You'll go to your grave without ever having been any better. When are you going to be whole?"

She thought about that for a minute and then she **said out loud,** "When I *touch* His clothes, I shall be made whole. That's when I'll be made whole." She established a point of contact to release her faith.

She then began the process of building a faith image within her spirit. Keep in mind that *The Amplified Bible* says, "She kept saying." She didn't quit saying it.

Don't let the Word depart out of your mouth. Meditate therein day and night. Observe to do all that's written therein: Then *thou shalt make thy way prosperous, and then thou shalt have good success.* (Josh. 1:8.)

So she set out to get rid of that "grow worse" image by building an image of health, life, and strength. She did it by speaking faith-filled words.

God created this universe by speaking faith-filled words. The Bible says in Hebrews 11:3 that He framed the worlds by the Word of God. Faith-filled words framed this world. The Word of God will frame *your* world also, if you will begin to speak it continually.

That woman began to create a faith image in herself by saying, "When I touch His clothes, that's when it will happen." She was **changing the seen** and **shaping the unseen.**

When she touched His garment, *straightway the fountain of her blood was dried up; and she felt in her body that she was healed of that plague* (v. 29). The *last* thing that happened was *she felt in her body that she was healed.* Sometimes we want that to be first. We say, "If I *feel* it, I'll believe it. If I *see* it, I'll believe it." That's not the way it works.

Bad News

Remember, Jairus was with Jesus and the multitude. They were on their way to Jairus' house when all this happened. Verse 35 describes what happened next:

While he yet spake, there came from the ruler of the synagogue's house certain which said, Thy daughter is dead: why troublest thou the Master any further?

Here is Jairus' opportunity to let the words he has spoken depart and let fear come. But he has already built a faith image in himself by speaking those things in faith.

The Faith of Silence

As soon as Jesus heard what the runner said, He turned to Jairus and said, *Be not afraid, only believe* (v. 36).

Now look at what Jairus said:

"...................."

Nothing! Not one word.

God will take the things that are not and bring to naught the things that are.

There was Jairus. His little daughter was dead. But Jesus said, "Don't be afraid. Only believe."

Faith is the substance of things hoped for, or desired. Faith is the raw material, the spiritual raw material, from which things you desire are made.

Fear is the opposite force of faith. It is the substance of things not desired.

If you have fear, the thing you don't desire will come to pass.

Jairus didn't say anything. At this point, he took things he didn't say and brought to naught the things that were said. The word of faith had already been spoken: *She shall live.*

Jesus walked into that situation, and there was the little girl, dead. All the relatives were there, weeping and wailing, and He ran them all out — Grandma, Grandpa, Aunt Susie, Uncle LeRoy, all of them.

Listen to the words of Jesus: "She's not dead. She's asleep!" (v. 39, paraphrased).

Now wait a minute! She *is* dead, but Jesus said she's *not*. That sounds like a lie. But Jairus' words and his silence would not allow the death. **Bad news was destroyed by silence.**

Jesus is talking and acting in Kingdom principles. We must get an understanding of this if we are going to operate on the same level of faith. He is talking things that are not and speaking as though they were.

What is Jesus doing? He is not trying to convince them she is alive. That would be a lie because, naturally speaking, she is dead. He is effecting something by what He's saying. He is highly developed in the God-kind of faith.

Here is where some people are missing it. They say, "I started saying certain things, and nothing happened. I said it four or five days and it didn't come to pass." They are not developed in it.

Keep saying. Keep speaking. You're shaping the unseen. It doesn't come overnight; it is a process, a way of life.

The first thing your words are doing is causing faith to come. (Faith comes by hearing, and hearing comes by the Word of God.) You're really not going to effect many things until faith comes.

Speaking words builds an image inside you. It's shaping the unseen. It all goes back to seed-time and harvest. Anyone knows that if you plant *today,* you don't harvest *tomorrow.* Speaking words causes faith to come. Your words are like seeds: they will produce a harvest.

Jesus walked in and spoke to that dead girl, and she rose up! That was creative power flowing out His mouth because He was highly developed in Kingdom principles.

I want you to realize this is the way Jesus ministered in the earth. On every occasion **when He set out to change the seen, He absolutely would not talk about what was seen.** He would not consider the thing that was seen as being permanent, only temporary.

47

Speak The End Results

Take, for instance, in the 11th chapter of John, when the runner came and told Jesus, *He* (Lazarus) *whom thou lovest is sick* (v. 3).

After hearing that, Jesus said: *This sickness is not unto death, but for the glory of God, that the Son of God might be glorified thereby* (v. 4).

He did not say Lazarus' sickness was for the glory of God. Let me show you why you can't interpret it that way.

Jesus said, *This sickness is not unto death.* In the same sentence He said, . . . *but for the glory of God.* You must interpret all of that verse the same way. You can't change rules of interpretation in the middle of the sentence.

Jesus said, *This sickness is not unto death.* If you interpret that literally, you make Jesus a liar. But Jesus did not lie. He was speaking the end results. He would never let *death* in His mouth. He would never establish death as a fact upon anyone.

Later on, He said about Lazarus, "He died." (v. 14.) The *King James Version* states that He said, *Lazarus is dead*. But, according to the Greek, He didn't say that. It should have been translated, "Lazarus died." There is a big difference in someone who died and someone who is dead. If you don't believe that, look at Jesus: He died, but He isn't dead!

Lazarus had died, but Jesus didn't see him dead. Jesus looked beyond the bad news, beyond human emotions. To all outward appearances, He simply ignored what was presently in existence and spoke the end results.

What is He doing? He is shaping the unseen before He changes the seen.

Listen to His words:

Lazarus sleepeth.

I go, that I may awake him out of sleep (v. 11).

Thy brother shall rise again (v. 23).

I am the resurrection (v. 25).

Though he were dead, yet shall he live (v. 25).

Jesus said, *This sickness is not unto death, but for the glory of God.* In other words, "The ultimate end of this whole matter of sickness will not be *death;* the ultimate end of this whole matter *will bring glory to God."* It was the resurrection that brought the glory, not the sickness nor the death.

That's how Jesus shaped the unseen. When you study it, you'll find that all through the New Testament He operated in Kingdom principles. In fact, you will find this true of God from Genesis to Revelation.

In Genesis, chapter 1, God created by the spoken Word.

Revelation 12:11 says: *They overcame him by the blood of the Lamb, and by the word of their testimony.*

Someone may say, "I don't understand why some things happen. Why can't I overcome the way others do?"

Some people don't overcome because there is no Word in their testimony.

There is bad news in it, but no Word of God.

When Jesus arrived in Bethany, Lazarus' hometown, He was still working on shaping the unseen. When Jesus told the people to roll the stone away, Lazarus' sister said, *Lord, by this time he stinketh: for he hath been dead four days* (v. 39).

But Jesus raised His eyes toward heaven and said, *Father, I thank thee that thou hast heard me* (v. 41).

But wait a minute! He hasn't said anything yet — or has He?

Yes! Four days before, He said, "This sickness will not ultimately end in death." He has already established this with His own words. Let me paraphrase it:

"Father, I thank You that You heard what I proclaimed four days ago. I established it then. This thing is not going to end with death. And I *knew* that You heard Me. I know that You always hear Me. That is the reason I said it so boldly four days ago.

"I am saying this for the benefit of the people here so that they will know the principles of the Kingdom that I used to bring about this great miracle. Then they will believe that You sent Me."

He was shaping the unseen and He is about to change the seen. Jesus said, *Lazarus, . . .*

I can just see Peter say, "Oh, dear Lord. What's He doing now? He's talking to a dead man!" (He was embarrassed.)

But when Jesus said, . . . *come forth* (v. 43), all the embarrassment left immediately because **Lazarus came forth!**

You may be a little embarrassed sometimes at things you're saying, proclaiming, or confessing; but when the manifestation comes, the embarrassment will leave.

Your words will change the seen and shape the unseen if you use these principles of the Kingdom.

God said: *I create the fruit of the lips* (Is. 57:19).

6

Righteousness Speaks

In the 10th chapter of Romans, verses 4-10, the Apostle Paul gives some insight into these principles that Jesus used in shaping the unseen:

For Christ is the end of the law for righteousness to every one that believeth. For Moses describeth the righteousness which is of the law, That the man which doeth those things shall live by them.

But the righteousness which is of faith speaketh on this wise, Say not in thine heart, Who shall ascend into heaven? (that is, to bring Christ down from above:) Or, Who shall descend into the deep? (that is, to bring up Christ again from the dead.)

First Paul tells you what the righteousness which is of faith would *not* say:

"Who's going to bring Jesus back that He may touch me? I'd get healed if

Jesus would come and touch me. Who's going to reverse the process of death and put Him back in the grave and bring Him back on the earth in His physical body so that He can touch me and I can be healed?"

Verse 8 begins: *But what saith it?*

What saith the righteousness which is of faith?

As verse 8 continues, we see what the righteousness of faith would say: *The word is nigh thee, even in thy mouth, and in thy heart: that is, the word of faith, which we preach.*

Notice, *The word is nigh thee,* not far off. You take the Word of God, put it in your mouth, and you **shape the unseen.** The words of your mouth, based on God's Word, change the things you see.

Verse 9 says: *If thou shalt confess with thy mouth the Lord Jesus, and shalt believe in thine heart that God hath raised him from the dead, thou shalt be saved.*

When I confessed Jesus as my Lord, the outward circumstances were such that anybody standing around me then would have said, "Oh, he's lying. I know Jesus is *not* his Lord."

They were right. He was *not* my Lord when I said it; but *because I said it in faith, it came to pass.* **I was calling things that were not as though they were.** It changed my life, and I became the righteousness of God in Christ.

That's the way you were born again! That's the way you changed your life: by confessing, "Jesus Christ is the Lord of my life. I believe that God raised Him from the dead. I proclaim now that Jesus is Lord."

When you said that, Satan *was* lord; but *because* you said it and acted in faith, the righteousness which is of faith brought you into right standing with God.

The Decision Was Yours

You made a decision and *spoke it with your mouth* which changed the seen and shaped what you could not see. You were born of the Spirit of God, absolutely transformed and changed by faith and your confession.

Verse 10 says: *For with the heart man believeth unto righteousness; and with the mouth confession is made unto salvation.* That word *salvation* means more than just being saved. It means "deliverance, preservation, healing, and soundness."

You shape the unseen by faith-filled words. Even a sinner can do it. The lost man can shape his eternal destiny by his words. He can change the unseen to the seen. *If thou shalt confess with thy mouth the Lord Jesus, and shalt believe in thine heart that God hath raised him from the dead, thou shalt be saved* (Rom. 10:9).

Thou shalt be saved! That's what God's Word says about you. Why walk in defeat? Why walk in the devil's territory when God's Word has been spoken?

But what will you say?

The devil has tried to con us into believing it won't work on anything else; but that's not true!

Just as Abraham and Sarah changed the seen and shaped the unseen with their words, based on what God said, so *your* words, based upon the authority of God's Word, can change the seen forces around you!

You don't have to accept what you see now. You don't have to go through life with the things that are now seen, for things that are seen are temporal — they are subject to change.

The decision *is* yours!

Charles Capps is a former farmer and land developer who travels throughout the United States, teaching and preaching God's Word. He shares from practical, first-hand experience how Christians can apply the Word to the circumstances of life and live victoriously.

Besides authoring several books, including the best-selling *The Tongue, A Creative Force*, Charles also has a nationwide radio ministry called "Concepts of Faith."

Charles and his wife Peggy make their home in England, Arkansas. Both their daughters, Annette and Beverly, are involved in full-time ministry.

For a complete list of tapes and books
by Charles Capps, write:

Charles Capps Ministries
P. O. Box 69
England, AR 72046

*Feel free to include your prayer requests
and comments when you write.*

BOOKS BY CHARLES CAPPS

Angels

The Tongue A Creative Force

Success Motivation Through The Word

Releasing the Ability of God
Through Prayer

Authority In Three Worlds

Can Your Faith Fail?

God's Creative Power
Will Work For You
(also available in Spanish)

God's Image of You

Dynamics of Faith & Confession

Hope — A Partner to Faith

How to Have Faith in Your Faith

How You Can Avoid Tragedy

Kicking Over Sacred Cows

Seedtime and Harvest

The Light of Life

The Substance of Things

Available at your local bookstore.

Harrison House

P.O. Box 35035 • Tulsa, OK 74153

HARRISON H⊕USE

BEST-SELLING BOOKS

Available at better book-stores everywhere.

Use your VISA or MASTER-CARD and order your faith-building books that can change your world!

A BEST-SELLING
CHARLES CAPPS BOOK

WHY TRAGEDY HAPPENS TO CHRISTIANS

How often have you heard the question: "They were such good Christians! Why did this happen to them?" Many believers' lives have been overwhelmed needlessly by defeat and tragedy.

Wrong speaking, wrong praying, and wrong believing will destroy your faith. Praying "If it be Thy will" has opened many doors for the devil's opportunity when God's will is already revealed in His Word.

This book was written to free you and to help you avoid tragedy in your life. Once you taste victory, you will never again have a desire to experience defeat. You can learn to apply the principles of God's wisdom to your life and defeat the devil.

Available at your local bookstore.